core belief™
Bible Study Series
for senior high

WHY Love MATTERS

Loveland, Colorado

Why Love Matters

Core Belief Bible Study Series

Credits

Editor: Karl Leuthauser
Creative Development Editors: Paul Woods and Ivy Beckwith
Chief Creative Officer: Joani Schultz
Copy Editor: Janis Sampson
Art Director: Ray Tollison
Cover Art Director: Jeff A. Storm
Computer Graphic Artist: Eris Klein
Photographer: Jafe Parsons
Production Manager: Gingar Kunkel

ISBN 0-7644-0889-5

10 9 8 7 6 5 4 3 2 1   07 06 05 04 03 02 01 00 99 98

Printed in the United States of America.

core belief

Bible Study Series
for senior high

contents:

the Core Belief: ▼Love

The word "love" in our culture signifies anything from the deepest affections we feel for others to an affinity for chocolate. We need to challenge ourselves to discover the true meaning of the word—an attitude involving action, commitment, and sacrifice. This Core Christian Belief challenges kids to discover this true meaning as it applies to God the Father's love for Christ and the Holy Spirit and to God's self-sacrificing love for people. Studies in this Core Christian Belief also challenge kids to explore how God's love for us should impact our love for him and for others.

the ▼Helpful Stuff

the ▼Studies

▼Love as a Core Christian Belief

Kids today hear a lot about love—from their friends, from movies, and from television. However, what they hear from those sources is often distorted. In the world's terms, love could be a warm feeling of infatuation for another person or an obsession with pizza. This ambiguity can lead people to do all sorts of immoral or hurtful things in the name of love.

However, the Bible's depiction of love is clear. It speaks of passion, sacrifice, and concern for others. It tells of the fantastic love God has for us—and what that love prompted him to do.

That's why this Core Christian Belief can make a difference in your young people's lives. Developing an accurate, biblical view of love can help your kids understand God better, learn to love him more, and put real love to work in their lives and relationships. When they begin to do those things, they'll truly experience what God and his love are all about.

Many kids have learned from society's example that love does not endure—people "fall" in and out of love on a daily basis. By helping kids discuss **divorce** and real love, the first study in this book will remind kids that God's love never fails—even in confusing and horrible circumstances.

The second study will help kids see that biblical love has no conditions. Kids will define real **love** and be encouraged by the example of Christ's life, which shows us that real love is a free gift.

In the third study, kids will be challenged to evaluate relationships according to the standards of real love. Kids will be taught to use love as a guide for **dating** as you remind them that God's Word shows them real love.

Finally, kids will examine some of the things in our world that people use as **substitutes for love.** These can include everything from drug or alcohol addiction to the use of pornography. Kids will learn to discern between real love and love substitutes, and they'll come to understand the destructive power of substitutes for love.

Love is the quality that shows others we are Jesus' followers. It's what makes friendships, families, and marriages work. It's what prompts people to serve and obey God. And it's what motivates us to share with other people what God has done for us. Love is what makes Christianity a faith of action and not just words.

*For a more comprehensive look at this Core Christian Belief, read Group's **Get Real: Making Core Christian Beliefs Relevant to Teenagers.***

DEPTHFINDER

HOW THE BIBLE DESCRIBES LOVE

To help you effectively guide your kids in this Core Christian Belief, use these overviews as a launching point for a more in-depth study of love.

- **God the Father's Love for Christ and the Holy Spirit**—Though we don't know many details about the inner relationship between the Father, the Spirit, and Jesus Christ, we know it's one of love. God the Father loves Jesus the Son much as a human parent loves his or her own child, and Jesus loves the Father as well. The Holy Spirit provides the bond of oneness and unity between them. That love relationship has existed since before time began; it's part of the nature of God, and is demonstrated for us throughout Jesus' life on earth (Matthew 17:5; John 14:31; 17:24; Colossians 1:13; 1 John 4:16).

- **God's Love for Humanity**—Though human nature leads people toward loving themselves instead of God, God's nature is to love people. Not many people have the courage to really love someone who totally rejects them. But that's the kind of love God shows for us.

  In the Old Testament, God's love is directed primarily at Israel. That love, however, is a personal love, compared to a mother's love for her baby. It's also seen as an eternal love, enduring even human rejection.

  In the New Testament, God's love is directed toward the whole world, but more specifically toward individuals than to any group of people. God's love is shown most effectively through the life of Christ. Though he sometimes spoke of the Father's love for us, he more often demonstrated God's love by helping and healing people. His ultimate act of love was sacrificing his own life for the sake of the world (Deuteronomy 6:4-5; Isaiah 49:14-15; John 3:16; Mark 1:40-42; Romans 5:6-8; Galatians 2:20).

- **Our Love for God**—When God gave the Law at Sinai, he commanded the Israelites to love him. However, our natural tendency is to love ourselves and not God. The Israelites were never able to maintain their love for God for very long. Nevertheless, God is still passionately drawing people to love him. Part of demonstrating our love for God involves loving other people. In fact, the Bible states that if we don't love others, we don't really love God (Deuteronomy 11:1; Matthew 6:24; 22:37; John 14:23-24; 1 John 4:7-21).
- **Our Love for Others**—Our love for other people should grow naturally out of our love for God. Jesus encourages us to love one another as he loved us. That love should be directed not only to other Christians, but also to anyone who's in need—including our enemies.

Another part of human love involves the romantic love between a man and a woman. This unique expression of love can be best defined by its desire to forge a lifelong, sacrificial relationship with the other person. Despite this unique quality, husbands and wives must also follow the Bible's guidelines about love between any two people (Genesis 2:24; Song of Songs 1–8; Matthew 5:43-46; Luke 10:25-37; John 13:35; Galatians 6:10; Ephesians 5:33; 1 Corinthians 13; James 2:8-9, 14-17; 1 John 4:7).

CORE CHRISTIAN BELIEF OVERVIEW

Here are the twenty-four Core Christian Belief categories that form the backbone of Core Belief Bible Study Series:

The Nature of God	Jesus Christ	The Holy Spirit
Humanity	Evil	Suffering
Creation	The Spiritual Realm	The Bible
Salvation	Spiritual Growth	Personal Character
God's Justice	Sin & Forgiveness	The Last Days
Love	The Church	Worship
Authority	Prayer	Family
Service	Relationships	Sharing Faith

Look for Group's Core Belief Bible Study Series books in these other Core Christian Beliefs!

about

core belief

Bible Study Series
for senior high

Think for a moment about your young people. When your students walk out of your youth program after they graduate from junior high or high school, what do you want them to know? What foundation do you want them to have so they can make wise choices?

You probably want them to know the essentials of the Christian faith. You want them to base everything they do on the foundational truths of Christianity. Are you meeting this goal?

If you have any doubt that your kids will walk into adulthood knowing and living by the tenets of the Christian faith, then you've picked up the right book. All the books in Group's Core Belief Bible Study Series encourage young people to discover the essentials of Christianity and to put those essentials into practice. Let us explain...

What Is Group's Core Belief Bible Study Series?

Group's Core Belief Bible Study Series is a biblically in-depth study series for junior high and senior high teenagers. This Bible study series utilizes four defining commitments to create each study. These "plumb lines" provide structure and continuity for every activity, study, project, and discussion. They are:

● **A Commitment to Biblical Depth**—Core Belief Bible Study Series is founded on the belief that kids not only *can* understand the deeper truths of the Bible but also *want* to understand them. Therefore, the activities and studies in this series strive to explain the "why" behind every truth we explore. That way, kids learn principles, not just rules.

● **A Commitment to Relevance**—Most kids aren't interested in abstract theories or doctrines about the universe. They want to know how to live successfully right now, today, in the heat of problems they can't ignore. Because of this, each study connects a real-life need with biblical principles that speak directly to that need. This study series finally bridges the gap between Bible truths and the real-world issues kids face.

● **A Commitment to Variety**—Today's young people have been raised in a sound bite world. They demand variety. For that reason, no two meetings in this study series are shaped exactly the same.

● **A Commitment to Active and Interactive Learning**—Active learning is learning by doing. Interactive learning simply takes active learning a step further by having kids teach each other what they've learned. It's a process that helps kids internalize and remember their discoveries.

For a more detailed description of these concepts, see the section titled "Why Active and Interactive Learning Works With Teenagers" beginning on page 57.

So how can you accomplish all this in a set of four easy-to-lead Bible studies? By weaving together various "power" elements to produce a fun experience that leaves kids challenged and encouraged.

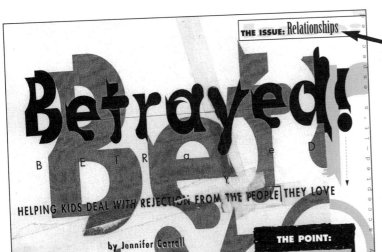

THE ISSUE: Relationships

Betrayed!

HELPING KIDS DEAL WITH REJECTION FROM THE PEOPLE THEY LOVE

by Jennifer Carrell

THE POINT:

God is love.

■ Betrayal has very little shock value for this generation. It's as commonplace as compact discs and mosh pits. For many kids today, betrayal characterizes their parents' wedding vows. It's part of their curriculum at school; it defines the headlines and evening news. Betrayal is not only accepted—it's expected. ■ At the heart of such acceptance lies the belief that nothing is absolute. No vow, no law, no promise can be trusted. Relationships are betrayed at the earliest convenience. Repeatedly, kids see that something called "love" lasts just as long as it's ... permanence. But deep inside, they hunger to see a

The Study
AT A GLANCE

SECTION	MINUTES	WHAT STUDENTS WILL DO	SUPPLIES
Discussion Starter	up to 5	JUMP-START—Identify some of the most common themes in today's movies.	Newsprint, marker
Investigation of Betrayal	12 to 15	REALITY CHECK—Form groups to compare anonymous, real-life stories of betrayal with experiences in their own lives.	"Profiles of Betrayal" handouts (p. 20), highlighter pens, newsprint, marker, tape
	3 to 5	WHO BETRAYED WHOM?—Guess the identities of the people profiled in the handouts.	Paper, tape, pen
Investigation of True Love	15 to 18	SOURCE WORK—Study and discuss God's definition of perfect love.	Bibles, newsprint, marker
	5 to 7	LOVE MESSAGES—Create unique ways to send a "message of love" to the victims of betrayal they've been studying.	Newsprint, markers, tape
Personal Application	10 to 15	SYMBOLIC LOVE—Give a partner a personal symbol of perfect love.	Paper lunch sack, pens, scissors, paper, catalogs

notes:

Betrayed!   16

Permission to photocopy this page from Group's Core Belief Bible Study Series granted for local church use.
Copyright © Group Publishing, Inc., Box 481, Loveland, CO 80539.

● **A Relevant Topic**—More than ever before, kids live in the now. What matters to them and what attracts their hearts is what's happening in their world at this moment. For this reason, every Core Belief Bible Study focuses on a particular hot topic that kids care about.

● **A Core Christian Belief**—Group's Core Belief Bible Study Series organizes the wealth of Christian truth and experience into twenty-four Core Christian Belief categories. These twenty-four headings act as umbrellas for a collection of detailed beliefs that define Christianity and set it apart from the world and every other religion. Each book in this series features one Core Christian Belief with lessons suited for junior high or senior high students.

"But," you ask, "won't my kids be bored talking about all these spiritual beliefs?" No way! As a youth leader, you know the value of using hot topics to connect with young people. Ultimately teenagers talk about issues because they're searching for meaning in their lives. They want to find the one equation that will make sense of all the confusing events happening around them. Each Core Belief Bible Study answers that need by connecting a hot topic with a powerful Christian principle. Kids walk away from the study with something more solid than just the shifting ebb and flow of their own opinions. They walk away with a deeper understanding of their Christian faith.

● **The Point**—This simple statement is designed to be the intersection between the Core Christian Belief and the hot topic. Everything in the study ultimately focuses on The Point so that kids study it and allow it time to sink into their hearts.

● **The Study at a Glance**—A quick look at this chart will tell you what kids will do, how long it will take them to do it, and what supplies you'll need to get it done.

Helpful Stuff   11

● **The Bible Connection**—This is the power base of each study. Whether it's just one verse or several chapters, The Bible Connection provides the vital link between kids' minds and their hearts. The content of each Core Belief Bible Study reflects the belief that the true power of God—the power to expose, heal, and change kids' lives—is contained in his Word.

THE POINT OF *BETRAYED!*:

God is love.

THE BIBLE CONNECTION

| 1 JOHN 4:7-21 | The Apostle John explains the nature and definition of perfect love. |

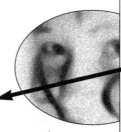

In this study, kids will compare the imperfect love defined in real-life stories of betrayal to God's definition of perfect love.

By making this comparison, kids can discover that God is love and therefore incapable of betraying them. Then they'll be able to recognize the incredible opportunity God offers to experience the only relationship worthy of their absolute trust.

Explore the verses in The Bible Connection and the information in the Depthfinder boxes throughout understanding of how these Scriptures con

LEADER TIP for The Study

THE STUDY

DISCUSSION STARTER ▼

Jump-Start (up to 5 minutes) As kids arrive, ask them to thi common themes in movies, books, TV sho have kids each contribute ideas for a ma two other kids in the room and sharing sider providing copies of People magazine what's currently showing on television or at their suggestions, write their respon on n **come up with a lot of great ideas. Even th ent, look through this list an try to disc ments most of these theme have in com

After kids make several s gestions, ment responses are connected the idea of bet

● **Why do you think** etrayal is such a

Betrayed! 17

LEADER TIP for The Study

Because this topic can be so powerful and relevant to kids' lives, your group members may be tempted to get caught up in issues and lose sight of the deeper biblical principle found in The Point. Help your kids grasp The Point by guiding kids to focus on the biblical investigation and discussing how God's truth connects with reality in their lives.

DEPTHFINDER UNDERSTANDING INTEGRITY

Your students may not be entirely familiar with the meaning of integrity, especially as it might apply to God's character in the Trinity. Use these definitions (taken from Webster's II New Riverside Dictionary) and other information to help you guide kids toward a better understanding of how God maintains integrity through the three expressions of the Trinity.

Integrity: 1. Firm adherence to a code or standard of values. 2. The state of being unimpaired. 3. The quality or condition of being undivided.

Synonyms for integrity include probity, completeness, wholeness, soundness, and perfection.

Our word "integrity" comes from the Latin word *integritas*, which means soundness. *Integritas* is also the root of the word "integer," which means "whole or complete," as in a "whole" number.

The Hebrew word that's often translated "integrity" (for example, in Psalm 25:21 [NIV]) is *tam*. It means whole, perfect, sincere, and honest.

CREATIVE GOD-EXPLORATION ▼

Top Hats (18 to 20 minutes) Form three groups, with each trio member from the previous activity going to a different group. Give each group Bibles, paper, and pens, and assign each group a different hat God wears: Father, Son, or Holy Spirit.

● **Depthfinder Boxes**—These informative sidelights located throughout each study add insight into a particular passage, word, historical fact, or Christian doctrine. Depthfinder boxes also provide insight into teen culture, adolescent development, current events, and philosophy.

h_{oly} Profiles

Your assigned Bible passage describes how a particular person or group responded when confronted with God's holiness. Use the information in your passage to help your group discuss the questions below. Then use your flashlights to teach the other two groups what you discover.

■ Based on your passage, what does holiness look like?

■ What does holiness sound like?

■ When people see God's holiness, how does it affect them?

■ How is this response to God's holiness like humility?

■ Based on your passage, how would you describe humility?

■ Why is humility an appropriate human response to God's holiness?

■ Based on what you see in your passage, do you think you are a humble person? Why or why not?

■ What's one way you could develop humility in your life this week?

● **Leader Tips**—These handy information boxes coach you through the study, offering helpful suggestions on everything from altering activities for different-sized groups to streamlining discussions to using effective discipline techniques.

● **Handouts**—Most Core Belief Bible Studies include photocopiable handouts to use with your group. Handouts might take the form of a fun game, a lively discussion starter, or a challenging study page for kids to take home—anything to make your study more meaningful and effective.

The Last Word on Core Belief Bible Studies

Soon after you begin to use Group's Core Belief Bible Study Series, you'll see signs of real growth in your group members. Your kids will gain a deeper understanding of the Bible and of their own Christian faith. They'll see more clearly how a relationship with Jesus affects their daily lives. And they'll grow closer to God.

But that's not all. You'll also see kids grow closer to one another.

That's because this series is founded on the principle that Christian faith grows best in the context of relationship. Each study uses a variety of interactive pairs and small groups and always includes discussion questions that promote deeper relationships. The friendships kids will build through this study series will enable them to grow *together* toward a deeper relationship with God.

When the Vow Breaks

WHAT DIVORCE TEACHES YOUNG PEOPLE

by Jane Vogel

THE POINT:

God's love never fails you.

■ Children of divorce have a hard time in life. Compared to kids who don't come from divorced families, these kids are more likely to drop out of high school, struggle getting a job, or become teenage parents. ■ They live in a society in which marriage is a disposable commitment, and the fallout from their parents' choice plagues them with questions that won't go away: "Is anything in life unshakable?" "Will the ones I love always leave me?" "Is there anyone I can really depend on?" ■ Of course, you know the answer. ■ Do your young people? ■ This study takes kids on a trip through the Promised Land—to demonstrate how God's love can never fail them even when those they love most walk away.

The Study
AT A GLANCE

SECTION	MINUTES	WHAT STUDENTS WILL DO	SUPPLIES
Construction Project	15 to 20	TOPOGRAPHERS 'R' US—Form teams to construct a room-sized topographical map of the land of Canaan.	Bibles, masking tape, scissors, paper, markers, assorted craft supplies, "This Land Is Your Land—Promise!" handouts (p. 23)
Promised Land Exploration	20 to 30	CLAIMING THE PROMISED LAND—Trace Joshua's journey and explore how God kept his promise to Joshua.	Bibles, "This Land Is Your Land—Promise!" handouts (p. 23)
Journey Reflection	up to 5	CLAIMING THE PROMISES—Discuss the impact of discovering that God makes the same promise to them as he did to Joshua.	Bibles
	5 to 10	STANDING ON THE PROMISED LAND—Stand on the map at the landmarks that represent where they are in their family lives now.	"This Land Is Your Land—Promise!" handouts (p. 23), newsprint, marker, tape

notes:

THE POINT OF "WHEN THE VOW BREAKS":

God's love never fails you.

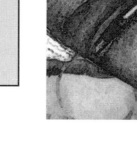

THE BIBLE CONNECTION

JOSHUA 1:1-9	God promises never to leave or abandon Joshua.
HEBREWS 13:4-6	God promises never to leave or abandon us.

I n this study, kids will compare the feelings of loss and abandonment Joshua felt at Moses' death to the feelings they experience when they cope with divorce. They'll explore the ways God kept his promise never to leave Joshua and discover that God makes the same promise to them.

By relating the promises in the Bible to their real-life experiences, kids can develop the confidence and courage to face whatever comes, secure in God's ever-present love.

Explore the verses in The Bible Connection, then examine the information in the Depthfinder boxes throughout the study to gain a deeper understanding of how these Scriptures connect with your young people.

BEFORE THE STUDY

In this study, teams of three will transform your meeting room into a topographical map of the Promised Land, using the handout "This Land Is Your Land—Promise!" Estimate how many teams of three you expect to form and photocopy enough handouts so that each person can have one.

Also, re-create the seven regions marked on your map by laying lines of masking tape onto your meeting-room floor. That will help kids transfer the information from the handout onto the classroom floor more easily.

Next, choose which supplies you'd like to provide for the transformation process. You can make this project as simple or as elaborate as you wish, depending on what you provide. Here are some ideas for useful supplies; choose as many or as few as you wish and add your own creative ideas:
- brown paper bags or newsprint (kids can use these to cover chairs to make mountains, draw pictures, create flat desert lands, and so on);
- stones (for altars, rocky areas, hills);
- colored construction paper;
- aluminum foil (for water);
- wood blocks, bricks, or cardboard blocks (for the tumbled walls of Jericho); and
- mothballs (for the hailstones that fell on Gibeon).

LEADER TIP for The Study

Because this topic can be so powerful and relevant to kids' lives, your group members may be tempted to get caught up in issues and lose sight of the deeper biblical principle found in The Point. Help your kids grasp The Point by guiding kids to focus on the biblical investigation and discussing how God's truth connects with reality in their lives.

When the Vow Breaks   17

LEADER TIP
for The Study

Whenever you ask pairs or groups to discuss several questions in a row, write the questions on newsprint, and tape the newsprint to the wall. That way groups can move through the discussion at their own pace.

LEADER TIP
for Topographers 'R' Us

Don't worry about your group's size being too small or too large to do this activity. If you have fewer than twenty-one kids, assign some groups more than one region to re-create. If you have more than twenty-one kids, give more than one group the same region to transform and have the groups work together.

THE STUDY

CONSTRUCTION PROJECT ▼

Topographers 'R' Us (15 to 20 minutes)
As kids arrive, form "topography teams" of three. Give each person a photocopy of "This Land Is Your Land— Promise!" (p. 23). (Tell kids to keep track of their handouts; they'll use them again later on.) Assign each team one region of the map and a corresponding section of the meeting room to turn into a three-dimensional topographical map using the supplies you've provided. Let kids know that later in the study they'll be leading tours of their areas, so they should look up any unfamiliar episodes listed for their regions from the handout now and be prepared to tell what happened.

While kids work, go around the room and ask teams to explain what part of the land they're creating and how it relates to Joshua's life. If kids aren't familiar with Joshua's story, take this opportunity to familiarize kids with the stories they'll be studying in detail later.

PROMISED LAND EXPLORATION ▼

Claiming the Promised Land (20 to 30 minutes)
When all the teams are finished with their regions, gather at the starting point (see the handout) on the bank of the Jordan River. Distribute Bibles, then say: **Today we're going to talk about divorce and explore how it affects the way we live. To do that, we're going to go on an exploration of a very old land— the "Promised Land" you've created here.**

Have kids open their Bibles to Joshua 1:1-9. Then say: **I'm going to read aloud Joshua 1:1-9. This episode takes place after Moses had**

DEPTH FINDER DIVORCE AND YOUNG PEOPLE

Today's teenagers have grown up in an era in which about one out of every two marriages ends in divorce. But the fact that divorce is so common doesn't make it any less painful. Judith Wallerstein, a clinical psychologist who studied 131 children of divorce for a span of fifteen years, "found them to be at higher risk for depression, poor grades, substance abuse, and intimacy problems."

Even if the kids you know don't seem to have those problems, don't assume they've dealt with their parents' divorces and moved on. Wallerstein says that when she did follow-up studies on kids eighteen months after their parents' divorces, "We didn't see a single child to whom divorce was not the central event of their lives."

When the Vow Breaks 18

led the people of Israel out of slavery in Egypt and after he had led them through the wilderness for forty years. Moses had been a very important person to the people of Israel. As you follow along in your Bibles, every time I read the name "Moses," I want you to repeat his name in a loud wail, as if you were the Israelites mourning his death. Every time I read the words, "Be strong and courageous," shout out that phrase.

Read the passage aloud, cuing the kids as needed. Then ask:

● If you'd been Joshua, how would you have felt about losing your hero and leader, Moses?

● In what ways might it have seemed that Moses and maybe even God had failed Joshua?

● Why did Joshua need to be strong and courageous?

● If you had been Joshua, would you have believed all the promises God was making here? Why or why not?

● How are the feelings you have when your parents (or a friend's parents) divorced like the feelings Joshua had when Moses died?

● In what ways does it seem like parents and maybe even God have failed you when your parents break up?

● When you're coping with divorce, what challenges do you face that require strength and courage?

● In rough times like that, how easy is it for you to believe God's promise that <u>God's love never fails you</u>?

Say: **Let's follow Joshua's route and see whether God kept his promises to Joshua. As a group, walk along the route Joshua took as shown on the handout. Stop at each landmark, and have a member of that region's team explain what happened.**

At each stop, have kids find a partner and discuss these questions:

● **What circumstances in this situation required strength and courage?**

● **How did God demonstrate that he was with Joshua in this situation?**

LEADER TIP for Claiming the Promised Land

If many of your students have not struggled with divorce in their own families or a family close to them, you can broaden this topic by asking kids to reflect on any ways they've felt abandoned.

LEADER TIP for Claiming the Promised Land

If you have more than twenty students, or your meeting room is small, you may prefer not to have all the kids explore the Promised Land as one group. As an option, you can form three groups by having members of each topography team number off, then cluster with other kids according to their assigned numbers. Assign each group an adult volunteer, then have groups follow each other through the exploration of the topographical map.

DEPTH FINDER — WHEN DIVORCE IS A RELIEF

"If you were divorced, you wouldn't fight. I wish you were divorced," wrote one young person in a therapy group for children whose parents had filed for divorce.

Some kids are glad when their parents divorce, particularly when physical abuse or substance abuse has been a problem. These kids may not grieve for the absent parent or wish their parents were back together, but they share the feelings of abandonment and betrayal that other children of divorce experience. For these kids, the sense of loss is not that a once-happy family has been broken apart, but that they never had a happy family.

So when kids tell you they're glad their parents divorced, ask them to describe their *ideal* family and discuss how that differs from their real-life experience. This will help kids begin to recognize and work through the hurts caused by their parents' divorces.

● **How do you think this experience influenced Joshua's understanding that <u>God's love never fails</u>?**

When you reach the journey's end at the hills of Debir, read aloud Joshua 11:23b from the handout: **"Then the land had rest from war."**

Have kids turn to their partners and discuss these questions:

● **How do you think Joshua felt spending all that time in war?**

● **How is coping with divorce like being in a war?**

● **How does knowing that <u>God's love never fails you</u> help you be strong and brave, even if your parents divorce?**

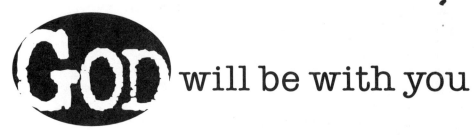

"Have I not commanded you? Be **strong** & courageous. Do not be terrified; Do not be discouraged, for the Lord your **GOD** will be with you wherever you go."

JOSHUA 1:9

DEPTH FINDER
UNDERSTANDING THE BIBLE

How do you teach about God's love from a violent, war-filled book such as Joshua? What will you say when your students ask, "How could a loving God demand so much bloodshed?"

To understand the book of Joshua, we have to see how it fits into the big picture of God's relationship with his beloved people, Israel. With all the world around them refusing to acknowledge the true God, God consistently warned the Israelites not to be lured away from him to join in the worship of pagan gods. But because God knew how likely the Israelites were to be influenced by their pagan neighbors, he commanded them to drive out or destroy all sources of temptation to idolatry.

The war Israel waged on the Canaanites was more than a conquest for the land that had been promised to Abraham. It was evidence of God's desire to preserve Israel's purity in a loving relationship with God—rather than allow them to destroy themselves by worshiping false idols.

Despite this, your kids may argue, "But was it necessary to kill everyone, including babies and young children?" Future events showed that it was. God knew those people that Israel did not destroy would rise up in the future and become a terrible danger to Israel's faith and well-being. The book of Judges details the sad history of Israel's spiritual and physical downfall at the hands of people they failed to drive out of Canaan.

How does all this relate to your students today? The book of Joshua makes it clear that it was God, not the army, who fought the battles for Israel. When your students face the spiritual and emotional battles of coping with divorce, they can count on the unfailing love of God, who fights to keep his children free and close to his heart.

JOURNEY REFLECTION ▼

Claiming the Promises (up to 5 minutes)
Have kids get back in their original topography teams of three. Make sure everyone has a Bible.

Say: **In your threesome, have each person read aloud one verse from Hebrews 13:4-6, then discuss these questions:**

● **What would you say to someone who told you that God's promise to be with Joshua doesn't apply to us today?**

● **What have you learned from Joshua's experiences that can help you cope with the divorce of people you care about?**

Standing on the Promised Land (5 to 10 minutes)
Say: **Look again at the map. Choose the spot that best represents where you are in your family life right now. For example, you might choose the bank of the Jordan River because your family is facing a difficult obstacle that will take God's special help to overcome. Or you might choose a site of a battle if you feel like your family is always fighting or the hills of Debir if your family is**

having peace after some bad fights.

Encourage kids to look at the map on the handout to remember what all the landmarks are. Then say: **Once you've chosen the spot that best represents where you are, go stand there on our room map. When everyone is standing at a spot on the map, say: Now turn to the person closest to you on the map and share how your spot on the map represents your life right now.**

After kids share, say: **Now take turns praying for each other. When you pray, pray about these three things:**

● **ask God to give your partner strength and courage to face the challenges coming up,**

● **praise God for a specific way your partner has shown courage in facing challenges in family life, and**

● **thank God that <u>his love never fails you.</u>**

Write the prayer instructions on newsprint, and tape it to the wall. Then have kids pray together. After the prayer, say: **Choose an item from the map near you to take home with you. Place it next to your bed all this week as a reminder that no matter what happens in your family, <u>God's love never fails you.</u>**

This Land Is Your Land—Promise!

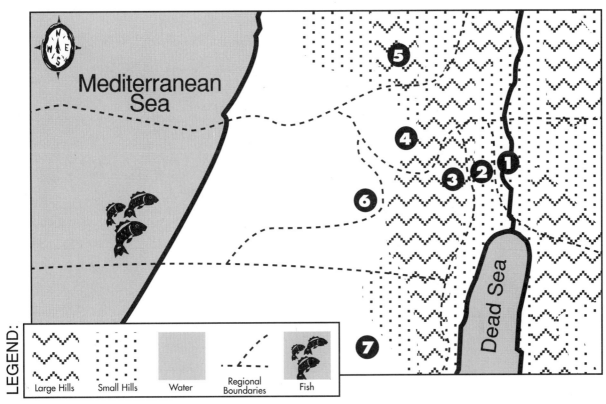

LEGEND:

Large Hills	Small Hills	Water	Regional Boundaries	Fish

1. JORDAN RIVER: God parted the river so the people could walk through on dry ground (Joshua 3).

2. JOSHUA built an altar to commemorate how God dried up the river (Joshua 4).

3. Jericho: The walls came a'tumbling down (Joshua 6).

4. Ai: The Israelites burned this enemy city to the ground (Joshua 8:1-29).

5. Mount Ebal: Joshua and the Israelites built an altar and renewed their commitment to God (Joshua 8:30-35).

6. Gibeon: God sent hailstones to defeat the enemy and made the sun stand still (Joshua 10:1-15).

7. Hills of Debir: "Then the land had rest from war" (Joshua 11:21-23).

if you love me, you'll...

Helping Kids Love Without Conditions

by Debbie Hanned

 Unconditional love is just an illusion. There are no free lunches here. No free rides. This is the land of "you scratch my back, and I'll scratch yours." It's called the law of give and take, and it rules this world. Everything has a price—from sneakers to education to the love of a gang. All you need to know is the cost. All you need to do is pay it. That is, if you can... ✖ They've been called the Bottomline Generation, and for good reason. Your students have learned to survive in a world where everything comes with a cost. Nothing is free, especially the things that really matter—such as friendship, belonging, and love. ✖ With their wizened, you-don't-get-something-for-nothing attitude, the very idea of "unconditional love" can sound ludicrous to today's teenagers. They might even call it dysfunctional. ✖ But for all their intellectual banter, their hearts all sound the same: *Love me! Love me! Love me! Love me!* ✖ This study guides kids to discover that unconditional love is real. It's theirs to receive from the One who loves them most and theirs to give to each other and to a hurting world.

> **THE POINT:**
>
> ## Real love is a free gift.

The Study
AT A GLANCE

SECTION	MINUTES	WHAT STUDENTS WILL DO	SUPPLIES
Creative Experience	5 to 10	ARMS OF LOVE—Discuss the meaning of love while giving or receiving love from others in the group.	
Love Project	20 to 25	LOVE BANNERS—Create banners that describe the world's view of love and the Bible's view of love.	Bibles, heavy aluminum foil, permanent markers, streamers, tape, magazines
Love Lab	20 to 25	LOVE WITHOUT STRINGS—Show love to each other anonymously.	Heavy aluminum foil, tape, permanent markers, background music
Group Prayer	up to 5	LOVE CONTINUUM—Pray together for God to help them love others unconditionally.	

notes:

THE POINT OF "IF YOU LOVE ME, YOU'LL...":

Real love is a free gift.

THE BIBLE CONNECTION

| 1 SAMUEL 20:1-42 | This passage describes the unselfish love shared by David and Jonathan. |
| 1 CORINTHIANS 13:4-7 | Paul explains the qualities of real love. |

I n this study, kids will create banners that describe selfish and unselfish love, then give their love as a free gift based on what they learn.

By creating the banners and doing an act of genuine love, students can understand that they don't have to "perform" to be loved because real love is a free gift.

Explore the verses in The Bible Connection, then examine the information in the Depthfinder boxes throughout the study to gain a deeper understanding of how these Scriptures connect with your young people.

THE STUDY

LEADER TIP for The Study

Because this topic can be so powerful and relevant to kids' lives, your group members may be tempted to get caught up in issues and lose sight of the deeper biblical principle found in The Point. Help your kids grasp The Point by guiding them to focus on the biblical investigation and discussing how God's truth connects with reality in their lives.

CREATIVE EXPERIENCE ▼

Arms of Love  (5 to 10 minutes) Have kids form a circle, then have them number off by twos. Say: **Today we're going to talk about real and false love. You're going to discover how you can tell whether or not somebody who says, "I love you" really means it. To get us started, I want all the Ones to place your arms around the shoulders of the Twos on either side of you.**

Once kids are in position, have them remain that way throughout the following discussion time. Ask:

● **Do you feel like you know what love is? Why or why not?**

● **Have you ever believed someone loved you—only to discover he or she really didn't? Explain.**

LEADER TIP for The Study

Whenever groups discuss a list of questions, write the questions on newsprint, and tape the newsprint to the wall so groups can answer the questions at their own pace.

● **How would you know if someone who claimed to love you really didn't?**

● **Have you ever felt like you wouldn't be loved by someone unless you did what he or she wanted? Explain.**

● **Do you think people who withhold love that way really love you? Why or why not?**

Say: **People in real life sometimes attach "price tags" to their love. They require you to do things to "earn" their affection, or they withhold love until you behave the way they want you to.**

These relationships may seem like they're based on love, but they're really not. That's because <u>real love is always a free gift</u>.

Ask the Ones:

● **How does it feel to be giving a "free gift" of love to the people around you right now? Explain.**

● **How is this experience like giving genuine love in real life?**

Ask the Twos:

● **How does it feel to be receiving love from the people on either side of you?**

● **How is this experience like receiving genuine love in real life?**

Say: **<u>Real love is a free gift</u>. It carries no price tags, no punishment, no conditions. That's the kind of love we're going to talk about today.**

LEADER TIP for The Study

For added fun in this study, set up the chairs in the shape of a heart. Or create a large heart shape on the floor with tape, then have kids sit on the tape to form a heart-shaped circle.

LOVE PROJECT ▼

Love Banners (20 to 25 minutes) Form two groups, and have groups gather at opposite corners of the room. Set out heavy aluminum foil, permanent markers, streamers, and tape. Give one group Bibles and conservative magazines such as Family, Child, GROUP Magazine, and CCM Magazine. Give the other group only "popular culture" magazines such as People, Sassy, YM, GQ, and Rolling Stone. (Don't give Bibles to the second group.)

Have the Bible group use the supplies you've provided to create a "Real Love" banner that describes love based on these passages: 1 Samuel 20:1-42 and 1 Corinthians 13:4-7. Have the other group create a "Worldly Love" banner that describes love based solely on the magazines you've given them.

Ask both groups to use the foil to make their banners, then hang them vertically in their assigned corners. Encourage kids to decorate their banners by finding or drawing pictures, writing poems or phrases, and using signs or symbols that identify their assigned love.

When groups are finished, have kids each find a partner from the other group. Have pairs tell each other about their respective banners. Then have pairs discuss these questions:

● **What stands out to you the most about these two banners?**

● **Which kind of love are you most familiar with? Explain.**

LEADER TIP for Love Banners

To help kids understand the special love between David and Jonathan, consider giving each person a photocopy of the "True Friendship Love" handout (p. 32) to take home and study this week.

DEPTHFINDER
UNDERSTANDING THESE KIDS

In a culture in which the law of "give and take" is the norm, asking kids to buy into a love that's unconditional may actually strike them as "unhealthy" or "codependent." They might say unconditional love would be self-destructive or even self-abusive. After all, if you must love people unconditionally, what do you do if they start abusing you? Just forgive and stay with them?

If kids bring up this argument, make sure they understand the biblical distinction between "loving" someone and "having a relationship" with him or her.

The Bible never commands us to participate in any sort of unconditional relationship. That is, we're never told we have to be in a relationship with a particular person regardless of his or her behavior. As Christians, we have conditions set on all our relationships—with God (see Matthew 24:13; Mark 16:16; and John 10:9) and with others (see Matthew 18:15-17).

However, we are commanded to *love* others unconditionally. So if kids love people who begin to abuse them, they don't have to stay in relationships with those people. But they do have to keep loving them.

To help kids see how they can love people this way, have them consider their lives from God's perspective. He *loves* all the people in the world equally but has a *relationship* with a relative few.

● **Which kind of love are you the most drawn to? Explain.**
● **When have you seen an example of love that always comes with a price tag? of love that's always free?**

Have a volunteer read aloud 1 Corinthians 13:4-7. Then say:
Real love is a free gift. The Bible is full of examples of relationships that illustrate real love—the kind of love found in 1 Corinthians 13:4-7. For example, David and Jonathan shared a special friendship that was based on real love. They both had the power to manipulate others to get their way, but they chose not to. They turned away from false love and chose the real thing instead.

LOVE LAB ▼

Love Without Strings

(20 to 25 minutes)
Say: **To put all we've learned about real love into action, let's take time now to offer genuine, real love to each other.**

Gather kids around the Real Love banner and have three volunteers kneel in front of it with their backs to the group. Have other volunteers tape a sheet of aluminum foil to the back of each kneeling person. Ask the kneeling students to close their eyes.

Play music in the background—preferably about friendship or God's love. Then ask other students to come behind each kneeling student and use a permanent marker to write a characteristic of real love they see in that person. For example, kids might write, "You always care

LEADER TIP for Love Without Strings

If you have more than twelve students, you can streamline this activity by having kids form separate "love" groups of six or more, or by asking more than three volunteers to kneel at one time.

about people's problems" or "You give without expecting anything in return." Encourage kids to hug those who are kneeling if they want to but to be careful not to reveal their identities.

After the first three students have each been "loved" by most of the group, ask three more students to kneel. Begin the process over again and continue until everyone has been "loved."

Have kids remove the foil from their backs and read what others wrote. Then say: **These foil sheets are your personal "Love Banners." I encourage you to keep them—even frame them—to remind you of the love you show others and to remember that <u>real love is a free gift</u>.**

GROUP PRAYER ▼

Love Continuum (up to 5 minutes)

Ask:

- **Based on what we've learned so far, what kind of love do you desire?**
- **What kind of love do you give most often?**

Ask kids to choose a place to stand between the two banners according to which kind of love they feel from others most often. For example, if kids feel that most people love them conditionally, have them stand closer to the Worldly Love banner. Or if they feel that most people love them unconditionally, have them stand closer to the Real Love banner.

Once they're in position, say: **Look around. It seems that a lot** of us feel loved—or unloved—in the same ways. Turn to someone near you and tell that person one reason they're worthy to be loved unconditionally. Then kneel on the floor and pray together for God to teach you the secret of how to give <u>love to others as a free gift</u>.

Once kids are finished praying, dismiss the class.

"Love is patient, love is kind. It does not envy, it does not boast, it is not proud. It is not rude, it is not self-seeking, it is not easily angered, it keeps no record of wrongs. Love does not delight in evil but rejoices with the truth. It always protects, always trusts, always hopes, always perseveres."

—1 Corinthians 13:4-7

True Friendship

Love

Of all the relationships in the Bible, the friendship between David and Jonathan is often looked upon as a model of the pure, godly love all Christians should share with one another. And no wonder. These two men of God were willing to die for each other—and more.

In 1 Samuel 20, the Hebrew word translated "love" is *ahab*. In this passage, the word suggests the importance of not only feeling close to someone but also of treating them with honor, the way God would want them to be treated.

We can learn more about how to have this kind of love in our own lives by looking more closely at David and Jonathan's friendship. Read the Scripture verses listed on this page, and look for ways you can begin to develop friendships like the one that David and Jonathan shared.

- Jonathan comforts David. **1 Samuel 20:1-2**

- David is honest with Jonathan, even though what he's saying may be hard for Jonathan to handle. **1 Samuel 20:3**

- Jonathan believes David and is willing to do anything to help him. **1 Samuel 20:4**

- Jonathan is willing to risk his own safety to help David. **1 Samuel 20:5-13**

- Jonathan is willing to let David become king over Israel, even though Jonathan is the rightful heir. **1 Samuel 20:14-16**

- David makes a lifelong promise to show love to Jonathan and his descendants. **1 Samuel 20:17**

- Jonathan defends David before the king, who tries to kill Jonathan as a result. **1 Samuel 20:32-33**

- Even though Jonathan's life is threatened, he continues to be more concerned about David than himself. **1 Samuel 20:34**

- Jonathan warns David to flee, and they part in tears because of their love for each other. **1 Samuel 20:35-42**

Blind Dates
Helping Kids Go Into Relationships With Their Eyes Open

by Steve and Jenny Saavedra

■ One of the greatest pressures that teenagers feel today is to show success with the opposite sex. Most teenagers feel that dating relationships are unquestionably desirable and certainly worth significant time, energy, and devotion. A perusal through teenage magazines will quickly validate the truth of this claim; most contain several articles and quizzes on dating and how to obtain the ideal dating partner. Some of the magazines even promote the use of tarot cards and numerology as a way for teenagers to discover whether current love-interests are good matches. ■ In such a climate, teenagers may think that the Bible doesn't have any advice to offer them regarding dating. Kids often lack useful guidelines and criteria for their dating choices. ■ Fortunately, God has much to say about what real love is and how to recognize it. Teenagers don't need to stumble blindly through the nebulous world of dating, but instead can find guidelines in Scripture to help them. Once they discover what Christlike and loving relationships look like, they can begin to develop guidelines for making wise dating choices.

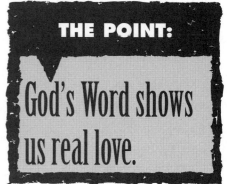

THE POINT:

God's Word shows us real love.

The Study
AT A GLANCE

SECTION	MINUTES	WHAT STUDENTS WILL DO	SUPPLIES
Creative Opener	10 to 15	CLASSIFIED LOVE—Read personal classified ads and discuss what these ads say about love, relationships, dating, and personal values.	Newsprint, marker, tape, "Looking for Love" handouts (p. 41)
Bible Exploration	25 to 30	SCRIPTURE SITCOMS—Identify characteristics of love mentioned in Scripture and create short television screenplays using the characteristics.	Bibles, paper, tape, newsprint, marker, index cards, pens
	5 to 10	INTERVIEW WITH A VENUS—Develop questions to use as criteria for choosing a person to date.	Bibles, "Interview With a Venus" handouts (pp. 42-43), pens
Creative Closing	5 to 10	CLOSING CLASSIFIEDS—Write a classified ad based on biblical definitions of love.	Handouts from the "Interview With a Venus" activity, pens

notes:

THE POINT OF "BLIND DATES":

God's Word shows us real love.

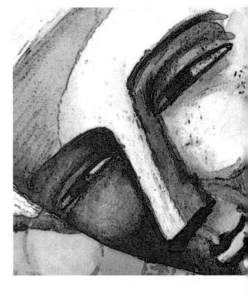

THE BIBLE CONNECTION

COLOSSIANS 3:12-14   These verses explain the importance of Christian love.

1 JOHN 3:16   This verse explains that real love is self-sacrificing.

I
n this study, kids will analyze personal ads and reflect on the understanding and definitions of love that the ads convey. They'll perform skits to demonstrate real-life beliefs about love and create personal standards and guidelines for perfect dating partners. Kids will then write their own personal ads using the standards they create.

Through these activities, kids can discover that God's Word shows us what real love looks like in the real world.

Explore the verses in The Bible Connection, then examine the information in the Depthfinder boxes throughout the study to gain a deeper understanding of how these Scriptures connect with your young people.

LEADER TIP for The Study

Because this topic can be so powerful and relevant to kids' lives, your group members may be tempted to get caught up in issues and lose sight of the deeper biblical principle found in The Point. Help your kids grasp The Point by guiding kids to focus on the biblical investigation and discussing how God's truth connects with reality in their lives.

BEFORE THE STUDY

For the "Classified Love" activity, write the following questions on a sheet of newsprint, and tape the newsprint to the wall:

● **Based on this ad, how do you think the writer of this ad would define real love?**

● **What seems to be the most important element in a relationship for this person?**

● **What does this ad say about this person's values?**

● **What does this person think brings happiness?**

THE STUDY

LEADER
TIP
for Classified Love

If your kids have trouble understanding the initials and abbreviations in the personal classified ads, explain the following key to them:

✓ B = black
✓ D = divorced
✓ F = female
✓ H = Hispanic
✓ H/W = height and weight
✓ LTR = long-term relationship
✓ M = male
✓ N/Drugs = no drugs
✓ N/S = nonsmoker
✓ S = single
✓ TLC = tender loving care
✓ W = white
✓ YO = year-old

CREATIVE OPENER ▼

Classified Love (10 to 15 minutes)

As kids arrive, have them form pairs, and give each pair a copy of the "Looking for Love" handout (p. 41). Say: **I'd like you to play the role of a psychologist. With your partner, carefully read the classifieds on your handout which were taken from a real newspaper. For each classified, your assignment is to analyze the writer's psyche and love life by discussing the questions posted on the wall. Be prepared to report your insights.**

Have kids discuss the four questions on the sheet of newsprint you prepared before the study. After about five minutes of discussion, ask a few volunteers to share some of their insights with the rest of the class. Then ask:

● **Where do people try to find love?**
● **What shapes our concept of love?**
● **Where do we learn about dating?**
● **What does society tell us about dating?**
● **How would you define true love?**
● **Do relationships bring true happiness? Explain.**

Say: **Although our family, peers, culture, and the media give us many powerful messages about love and dating, God's Word tells us about real love. When it comes to our "love lives," we often get so caught up in the expectations of others that we forget what the Bible tells us. It's impossible to be in a satisfying, happy, and lasting relationship if we don't exercise real love. So today we're going to try to discover what real love is.**

LEADER
TIP
for The Study

Whenever groups discuss a list of questions, write the questions on newsprint and tape the newsprint to the wall so groups can discuss the questions at their own pace.

BIBLE EXPLORATION ▼

Scripture Sitcoms (25 to 30 minutes)

Have kids return to their pairs. Give each pair a pen and a sheet of paper. Instruct pairs to read Colossians 3:12-14 and 1 John 3:16. Then have kids list on a sheet of paper the characteristics of love that the verses mention.

After a few minutes, call the class back together, and write the students' responses on a sheet of newsprint. Then say: **These characteristics from the Bible show us what God sees as real and perfect love. Using these characteristics, we are now going to put our creative minds together to create screenplays for television sitcoms that relate to dating and love.**

DEPTH FINDER

WHAT'S LOVE GOT TO DO WITH IT?

Some of your kids may find it difficult to make the connection between God's view of real love and their dating relationships. They may ask, "What does a serious consideration of love have to do with dating when I'm not even close to getting married?"

Help kids discover that understanding real love will give them a protective and beneficial standard for their relationships. When they find themselves in relationships that don't reflect biblical love, their knowledge of real love will set off warning signals and red flags, telling them that something's just not right. Being able to spot the difference between real love and empty love can save them from the hurt and scarring that unhealthy dating relationships can inflict.

All relationships go more smoothly when guided by God's standards of love. Your young people probably believe that sacrifice and trust are important qualities for friendships, but they may not apply these same expectations to dating. Kids may need a reminder that dating relationships should operate by the same rules as all relationships. A close study of what God sees as real love should help kids not only improve relationships with friends and family, but also with the opposite sex.

Finally, learning about and knowing how to recognize real love now will save them a lot of heartache down the road. Practicing real love in God-honoring dating relationships will prepare and mature them for "real courtship," which could be just around the bend.

Have kids form groups of three to five, and assign each group one of the characteristics of love listed on the newsprint. Then say: **Your job is to think of a TV personality who does *not* display your group's characteristic of love. Then choose another TV personality who you think would be an ideal date for your first choice. Create a short screenplay in two acts for these TV personalities. The first act should show how this couple relates *without* showing your love characteristic, and the second act should show how they would relate *with* your love characteristic. Be prepared to act these out for the class. Make certain every member in your group has a role.**

Give kids ten minutes to prepare their screenplays. While the groups are preparing, hand out index cards, pens, and tape so each group can make name tags for their TV personalities. When kids are ready, have each group perform both acts of its screenplay for the whole class.

Ask:

● **Which scene felt more natural to write and act out? Why?**

● **When your TV personalities operated by what God defines as real love, how did it make their lives different?**

● **How were the conflicts in your screenplays like those in real life?**

● **How does God's kind of love differ from the kind of love reflected in culture?**

● **How did you feel responding to a situation with God's kind of love?**

● **What do you think is the purpose of dating?**

● **What do you think is God's purpose for dating?**

LEADER TIP

for Scripture Sitcoms

If kids are unable to come up with appropriate television personalities, suggest that they consider movie and book characters or sports heroes.

● **How could God's view of real love impact teenage dating relationships?**

Say: **Because we live in a fallen world, we see and are affected by dysfunctional notions of love. Love is meant to be a beautiful thing, but people have tainted and twisted it. That's why it's so important for us to look to the source of real and true love. God's Word tells us what real love looks like. And looking to God as our source will make our human relationships much more fulfilling.**

LEADER TIP

for Interview With a Venus

If your kids are having a hard time thinking of questions to write down, help them get started by suggesting a few of the questions from the "Is This One Right for Me?" Depthfinder on this page.

Interview With a Venus   (5 to 10 minutes)

Give each student a copy of the "Interview With a Venus" handout (pp. 42-43). Say: **Imagine that you're going to be a participant in a dating game show called *Love's Perfection*. In this hypothetical game show, you get to ask three contestants of the opposite sex questions to help you decide which contestant you want to date. Your handout lists three important categories for you to focus on—spirituality, personality, and interests. Consider all three while deciding on what kind of person you want to date. In the left-hand column, list spiritual qualities, personality traits, and the personal interests that you seek in an ideal date. In the right-hand column, write out questions that you would like to ask the dating candidates to see if they meet your requirements. As you write your characteristics and questions, refer to our notes on Colossians 3:12-14 and 1 John 3:16 written on the newsprint. And for further inspiration, check out 1 Corinthians 13.**

DEPTHFINDER   IS THIS ONE RIGHT FOR ME?

Ray E. Short, author of *Sex, Love, or Infatuation: How Can I Really Know?* offers teenagers fourteen key clues to help them distinguish between true love and false love. Consider using some of these questions to help kids think about their ideal date during the "Interview With a Venus" activity.

CLUE 1: What is your main interest in the other person? What attracts you most?

CLUE 2: How many things about the person attract you?

CLUE 3: How did the romance start?

CLUE 4: How consistent is your level of interest?

CLUE 5: What effect does the romance have on your personality?

CLUE 6: How did it end?

CLUE 7: How do you two view each other?

CLUE 8: How do others view you two? What's the attitude of friends and families?

CLUE 9: What does distance (long separation) do to the relationship?

CLUE 10: How do quarrels affect the romance?

CLUE 11: How do you feel about and refer to your relationship?

CLUE 12: What's your ego response to the other?

CLUE 13: What's your overall attitude toward the other?

CLUE 14: What is the effect of jealousy?

DEPTH FINDER

DATING CRITERIA: TRUE, FALSE, OR BOTH?

Seventeen magazine recently published "How to Choose a Boyfriend," by Carolynn Carreño. Although the article was intended for girls, the writer's advice could apply to both guys and girls. The criteria the author lists may prove helpful to your students in choosing people to date. If you have time, ask your young people what they think of the following statements. Ask them if they think the list below (adapted from the original article) is complete.

1. You like him/her.
2. You like him/her whether or not he/she is popular.
3. You like the way he/she sees you.
4. You act like yourself around him/her, only better.
5. You feel like he/she respects you.
6. You have stuff in common.
7. You absolutely trust him/her.
8. You have high expectations of him/her.
9. You think he's/she's nice.
10. You more or less like his/her friends.
11. You can say anything to him/her.
12. He/She makes you happy.

Give kids enough time to finish at least two questions for each category. When kids are finished, tell them to find a partner and share their ideal characteristics and questions with each other. Have each pair discuss:

● **Why is it important for us to look at what God has to say about real love?**

● **How do your ideal dates as outlined on your handouts reflect God's perspective of real love?**

● **Explain how today's study might influence the way you go about choosing a date.**

Say: **In your dating experiences, it can be easy to get wrapped up in the idea of just having a boyfriend or girl-friend. But each of you have just written qualities that you and God think are more important than anything else in a dating relationship. Keep these questions and characteristics that you wrote down in a place where you can look at them occasionally. Use this handout as a way to help yourself choose when and when not to date a certain person.**

CREATIVE CLOSING ▼

Closing Classifieds (5 to 10 minutes)
Tell kids to exchange their "Interview With a Venus" handouts with their partners. Then say: **Your final task is to write a personal classified ad. For the beginning of the ad, write an opening description of your partner on his or her handout.**

When you do this, list several positive traits that you admire in him or her. For example, you might write, "Beautiful, gentle, sports-loving single Hispanic female…" Then when each partner is finished with this first part, exchange handouts once again, and complete the ads with a description of what you're personally looking for—or will be looking for—in a date. For example, "…seeks a patient, self-sacrificing, God-fearing, book lover." By doing this, you'll create a concise personal classified that expresses the qualities of biblical love you hope for in a date.

Give kids a few minutes to write the classifieds. Then say: **Love is a wonderful part of God's creation and <u>God's Word shows us what it should look like</u>.** Not only does God's Word give us important guidelines for choosing dating partners, it also tells us how we should treat those close to us. It's important that we pursue people who care about the qualities of biblical love. Doing so helps us understand what real love is all about.

Ask kids to pray with their partners for wisdom and discernment as they go about choosing dating partners. Then close in prayer thanking God for revealing real love to us.

"This is how we know what love is: Jesus Christ laid down his life for us. And we ought to lay down our lives for our brothers."

—1 John 3:16

❤ LOOKING FOR LOVE ❤

INTER-RACIAL EXPERIENCE

Attractive DBF, 48, desires financially/emotionally secure DWM, 45-55, for fun times. Must be 6'2", H/W proportionate, N/S, N/Drugs, social drinker. Let's experience the better things in life together. Serious inquiries only.

SEEKING RELATIONSHIP

Romantic, warm, active, and financially secure SBM, 25, 6'2", 175lbs., seeks relationship with a S/DF, for movies, dinner, travel. Race unimportant.

REAL COWBOY

DWM, 34, 6'1", 230lbs., very honest, loves outdoors, horseback riding, fishing, hunting, seeks honest WF, 25-39 with same interests, for friendship and possible long-term relationship.

I'LL SHARE MY LIFE

Let's play kissey face. SWM, 6', teddy-bear Christian, lovable, loves home-type cooking. TLC, LTR, with sincere, slender to medium, non-wild lady, 34-54, good times and gentle love beyond measure.

SEEKING HISPANIC MALE

Mexican American, 44, attractive inside/out, honest, caring, loving, mother of a 10YO boy, live in El Paso but thinking to relocate with the right man (I'm an excellent listener!). Seeking SHM, looks unimportant. For possible marriage.

NO COUCH POTATO

DWF, 45, blonde/blue, 5'8", 125lbs., loves to have fun, hike, bike, likes to eat. If you can cook and share my lust for life, please answer my ad.

INTERVIEW WITH a Venus

You are a participant on the game show *Love's Perfection*. The producers have asked you to list the qualities you're looking for in an ideal date. During the show, you will have the chance to ask the contestants several questions to help you determine who to date. Use this handout to determine what you're looking for in a date and what qualities in a person are important to you.

In the left-hand column list the qualities. In the right-hand column list a question that can help you determine whether or not this person matches your standards. An example is given below.

As you write your qualities and questions, refer to Colossians 3:12-14; 1 John 3:16; and 1 Corinthians 13.

QUALITIES	QUESTIONS
SPIRITUALITY: Forgiving	"If your best friend told one of your secrets, how many days or weeks would it take for you to forgive him or her?"

QUALITIES	QUESTIONS
PERSONALITY:	
INTERESTS:	

Only the Real Thing
Helping Kids Find Love

by Siv M. Ricketts

■ The famous psychologist Abraham Maslow identifies love as one of five fundamental human needs. No one can reasonably dispute the assertion that love is an essential element to the human experience. But what is love? Is it found in a passionate night? Is it found in lifelong unity? Is love measured in feelings of excitement? Is it discovered through feelings of familiarity? ■ Your kids are looking for the answers. They know they need love, but they're not sure what it is or how to get it. Therefore, teenagers will often try to satisfy their need for love in many ways—through sex, materialism, perfectionism, pornography, and eating disorders, for example. In fact, they'll try just about anything that makes them feel satisfied, even temporarily, in their search for authentic love.

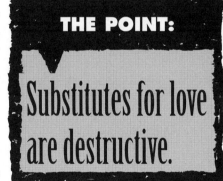

THE POINT:

Substitutes for love are destructive.

■ This study will help your kids begin to understand what real love is all about. It will show them why they need to pursue love that endures and why they must avoid damaging and painful substitutes.

The Study
AT A GLANCE

SECTION	MINUTES	WHAT STUDENTS WILL DO	SUPPLIES
Opening Experience	10 to 15	LOVE ME—Create and sell "dream offers," then discuss the price of substitutes for love.	Paper, pens
Bible Experience	15 to 20	LOVE SIMULATIONS—Decide whether certain characters should get involved in certain behaviors.	"Adam" handouts (p. 54), "Eva" handouts (p. 55), paper, pens
	10 to 15	REAL LOVE—Examine perspectives on love expressed in secular music, then look at biblical love.	Bibles, secular CDs or tapes, CD or tape player, newsprint, tape, marker
Closing Experience	5 to 10	STICKING TO LOVE—Pray for a friend who's been hurt by substitutes for love.	Adhesive bandages, markers

notes:

THE POINT OF "ONLY THE REAL THING":

Substitutes for love are destructive.

THE BIBLE CONNECTION

| ROMANS 5:6-8 | This passage describes how God showed his love for us. |
| 1 JOHN 4:7-12 | This passage explains real love. |

In this study, kids will discuss the price that comes with many substitutes for love, examine perspectives on love in popular media, and pray for others who have been hurt by love substitutes.

By doing this, kids can discover that many behaviors they and their friends consider normal are in fact manifestations of a search for love. They can find that substitutes for love bring destruction while real love brings healing.

Explore the verses in The Bible Connection, then examine the information in the Depthfinder boxes throughout the study to gain a deeper understanding of how these Scriptures connect with your young people.

BEFORE THE STUDY

For the "Real Love" activity, make the lyrics of one or two popular secular songs that express attitudes toward love available to your students.

LEADER TIP for The Study

Because this topic can be so powerful and relevant to kids' lives, your group members may be tempted to get caught up in issues and lose sight of the deeper biblical principle found in The Point. Help your kids grasp The Point by guiding kids to focus on the biblical investigation and discussing how God's truth connects with reality in their lives.

LEADER TIP

for The Study

Whenever groups discuss a list of questions, write the questions on newsprint and tape the newsprint to the wall so groups can discuss the questions at their own pace.

LEADER TIP

for Love Me

If students find that more than one person accepts an offer, have the seller "raise the price" by adding more troubles to the price tag until all but one person drops out of the bidding.

LEADER TIP

for Love Me

If it would take too long for each student to share, ask for a few volunteers, or have students form small groups and share with their group members. You may also choose to have teenagers discuss the debriefing questions in their groups.

THE STUDY

OPENING EXPERIENCE ▼

Love Me (10 to 15 minutes) Give each student a sheet of paper and a pen. Say: **In the next few minutes, you'll have a chance to create a "dream offer," then sell it to someone. For example, you could offer a beachfront mansion in Rio, complete with horse stables and a sports car. You can be as elaborate as you want, but you also need to include a hidden price tag. For example, with the mansion in Rio, you also get seventy-hour workweeks, a divorce, and a heart attack. Try to make the price tag appropriate to the offer.**

Allow students a couple of minutes to write their offers. Once the offers are written, tell students that they should sell them to each other by reading their descriptions. Explain that if someone shows interest in an offer, the seller should tell him or her the hidden price tag, and let the person decide whether the dream offer is actually worth the price. Instruct students to complete the deal by accepting the piece of paper on which the dream offer is written.

Each student must purchase only one offer, and each offer can only be purchased once. When everyone has purchased an offer, have each student explain what he or she bought and why.

Ask:

● **What things do people use as substitutes for love?**

● **What kind of hidden price tags go with those things?**

● **How does this activity show how people try to satisfy their need for love?**

● **Why do you think people chase after substitutes for love?**

● **What is real love like?**

Say: **As tempting as a beachfront mansion might be—when it comes at the expense of love—it's too expensive. In fact, substitutes for love are destructive. Now let's explore what substitutes for love might look like at your high school.**

BIBLE EXPERIENCE ▼

Love Simulations (15 to 20 minutes) Ask students to form groups of three or four with others of their own gender, and distribute pens and an "Adam" handout (p. 54) to each group of guys and an "Eva" handout (p. 55) to each group of girls. Say: **The handout you have has a description of either Adam or Eva, and four situations for each character. In your groups, read each situation and discuss the questions that**

DEPTH FINDER — UNDERSTANDING THESE KIDS

When families are acutely dysfunctional or moderately dysfunctional over time, family members often feel unloved and cope by assuming dysfunctional roles. In their book *Finding Hope for Your Home*, Dawson McAllister and Clark Albright address six common roles dysfunctional-family members fill. As substitutes for love, these roles are characteristically destructive, hindering people trapped in them from maturing and developing into the people that God intends them to be.

● **Scapegoats** take on the blame for their family's problems, whether or not the problems stem directly from their own behavior.

● **Rebels** act out their families' problems through destructive behavior because of their deep anger about what's happening within their families.

● **Heroes** believe that if they do enough things right, their families will stop fighting and be happier. Heroes often crack under the pressure of performance.

● **Clowns** use humor to distract themselves and others from the pain that surrounds them.

● **Lost Ones** are shadows, trying to keep both themselves and their deep anger and hurt hidden.

● **Fixers** try to produce peace by holding everyone and everything together.

These roles can lead to painful false beliefs such as "I'm totally alone"; "If I trust someone, I will be hurt"; "I am so bad I am unlovable"; and "God doesn't really care about me." Of course, God offers both love and healing to your students caught up in these roles. Psalm 27:10 says, "Though my father and mother forsake me, the Lord will receive me." There is hope with God.

If you sense that some of your teenagers are struggling with dysfunctional families and their roles within their families, share with them about their loving heavenly Father who has adopted them into his family. However, some teenagers have been so badly scarred that they may need professional counseling. If you haven't already, you might contact Christian counselors in your area who would be comfortable talking to these students on an individual basis.

follow. **The last question in each section can be answered yes, no, or undecided. Answer the last question silently, and keep track of your answer to the last question for each situation.**

Allow students ten to fifteen minutes to work through the situations. Call students' attention back to you and say: **Those of you who answered no to most of the last questions are probably pretty safe—though you might be tempted to substitute something for love. Those of you who answered undecided to most of the last questions are probably somewhere in the middle. You'll have to make up your mind sometime soon—hopefully before you find yourself in those situations. Those of you who answered yes to most of the last questions probably need to take a good look at where you go to find love. <u>Substitutes for love are destructive.</u> They take the place of what's real, and they never satisfy. In fact, they can tear you apart.**

Ask teenagers to form new small groups that include both guys and girls and discuss the following questions:

● **How do Adam's and Eva's situations demonstrate how people look to substitutes to meet their needs for love?**

LEADER TIP for Love Simulations

If time is short, you can choose to assign each group only one or two of the situations, and then have groups share what they discussed. In that case, you could ask students to quickly read through the other situations and silently answer the last question for each.

LEADER TIP

for Real Love

Your students can be an excellent resource in preparing for this activity. Call a couple of kids to find out which popular songs feature secular attitudes about love. They might let you borrow their CDs or tapes and might even type out the words for you. Whatever songs you use, make certain to check for offensive lyrics before you play them for the class.

● **What other things do teenagers substitute for love?**
● **Are those things destructive? Why or why not?**
● **Why do you think people settle for substitutes for love?**

Real Love (10 to 15 minutes)

Display the song lyrics you prepared before the study.

Say: **People have a real need for love. When that need isn't met, people turn to substitutes. And substitutes can be found everywhere in our culture. Popular music provides some excellent examples of love substitutes. I'm going to play a few songs, and I'd like you to identify the substitutes for love each song offers.**

Tape a sheet of newsprint to the wall. After you play each song, ask high schoolers to finish this sentence, "These songs tell us that love is…" while you write their responses on the sheet of newsprint.

Have kids form groups of four. Ask half of the groups to read

"This is love:

not that we loved God, but that he loved us and sent his Son as an atoning sacrifice for our sins."

DEPTH FINDER

WHAT IS LOVE ANYWAY?

Teenagers (and many adults) confuse love with romance or sex. Romance and sex are wonderful gifts that God has given couples to express love for each other. Used according to God's guidelines, romance and sex foster a sense of intimacy in an otherwise healthy relationship.

But romance and sex don't create love. Love is a God-given gift that we can choose to exercise. Love is proven by the committed and consistent choice to love others even when they appear, act, or are undesirable. Romance without love is merely a feeling of excitement. Sex without love is simply an act of self-gratification.

Romance and sex come and go; love endures. As Shakespeare says in Sonnet 116:

"Love alters not with [time's] brief hours and weeks,

But bears it out even to the edge of doom."

—1 John 4:10

DEPTH FINDER — CAN YOU FALL OUT OF LOVE?

How many times have you seen a character on television tell his or her spouse, "I just don't love you anymore." Popular culture suggests that people fall in and out of love all the time.

But it's *impossible* to fall out of love. The feelings that are often associated with love will most certainly come and go. People may or may not *feel* infatuation, romance, or desire for others whom they love. Warm and tender feelings cannot always be present in a relationship, but real love remains because real love is a choice.

1 Corinthians 13 shows how the choice to love is made manifest. When you love someone, you choose to be patient with him or her. You choose to be kind. You choose not to envy or keep a record of wrongs. You choose to protect, trust, and hope in the person.

We can't force ourselves to like everyone. We can't make ourselves feel amiable toward others. But we can choose to love everyone. It is impossible to fall out of love. But it is possible to choose to stop loving.

Romans 5:6-8 and the others to read 1 John 4:7-12. Have groups discuss:
- **According to this passage, why should we love one another?**
- **What does real love look like?**
- **What are some of the results of showing each other real love?**
- **What can help teenagers stay clear of substitutes for love?**
- **What are the differences between real love and substitutes for love?**

Tape another sheet of newsprint to the wall. Ask teenagers to complete the sentence, "These passages tell us that love is..." while you write their responses on a separate sheet of newsprint. Ask kids to point out the similarities and differences between the world's view of love depicted through the songs and God's view seen through his Word. During the week, type the two lists and distribute them at your next meeting.

Say: **Substitutes for love are destructive, but God's love offers forgiveness and hope through Jesus' death and resurrection. As we come to know and love God more and more, our love for ourselves and others will grow.**

LEADER TIP
for Sticking to Love

Consider providing colorful children's bandages. Tell your students that if their friends comment on the bandage, they can use the opportunity to share what they've learned through this lesson.

CLOSING EXPERIENCE ▼

Sticking to Love (5 to 10 minutes)
Pass out adhesive bandages and markers. Say: **If it's true that <u>substitutes for love are destructive</u>, then it should also be true that real love brings healing. Think about one person you know who has been hurt by a love substitute. Maybe he or she was caught up in some of the substitutes for love that we've talked about. Spend a moment in silent prayer for that person, asking God to heal your friend and to show you**

ways to express God's real love for him or her.

Give students a minute, then continue: **Now peel back the adhesive strips enough to see the bandage, and write your friend's initials on it. When you're done, stick the bandage to your hand to remind you to pray for your friend as long as it sticks to you. <u>Substitutes for love are destructive</u>, but God's love— real love—brings healing.** When kids are done, ask them to return to their small groups and each share one way he or she plans to express love differently as a result of this lesson.

"YOU SEE

at just the

right time,

when we were

still powerless, Christ died for the ungodly. Very rarely

will anyone die for a righteous man, though

for a good man someone might possibly dare to die. But

God demonstrated

his own love

for us in this:

While we were

still sinners,

Christ died

FOR US"

—Romans 5:6-8

Adam

Adam is seventeen years old and a senior in high school. His parents are married, but Adam doesn't think much of their relationship. His dad is tough and constantly tells Adam to "Be a man" and that "Real men don't express emotion." Adam can't recall the last time his dad told him he loved him. His mom, on the other hand, often tells him how much she loves him; however, she's so emotional, Adam gets embarrassed.

Situation 1: Adam's dad occasionally buys pornographic magazines. His mom doesn't know about them, but Adam found his dad's hiding place. He knows that pornography degrades women, but he's still tempted.
* What do you think would be the consequences of looking at the pornography?
* How might pornography affect Adam's perception of women? of real love?
* How can pornography be a substitute for love?
* Should Adam sneak a peak?

YES   NO   UNDECIDED

Situation 2: Adam and Kristi have been dating for six months. The big formal is coming up, and Adam's friends have rented a couple of hotel rooms to use after the dance. Adam thinks he and Kristi love each other, but he's not sure they're ready for sex. He also doesn't know how Kristi would feel about it. They've pushed the limits some, but they've never talked about it.
* How might Adam and Kristi's relationship change if they had sex?
* At what point in a relationship is it OK to have sex?
* How can sex be a substitute for love?
* Should Adam take Kristi to the hotel, assuming they'd have sex if he does?

YES   NO   UNDECIDED

Situation 3: Adam gets decent grades. He's also on the track team and has a part-time job at a fast-food place near school. He recently started selling ad space for the school newspaper (the paper needs the money to continue), and Adam just heard that the video store is hiring. He already makes enough money, but Adam thinks that maybe his dad will be proud if he sees how hard Adam works.
* What might be the consequences of taking on another job?
* How else could Adam get his dad to show him love?
* How can workaholism be a substitute for love?
* Should Adam take the job?

YES   NO   UNDECIDED

Situation 4: Recently some guys have been hanging out with Adam. Adam's pretty sure they're in a gang, but they're cool and really seem to want Adam around. They've invited him to go cruising Friday night, and it sounds like things could get wild. Adam feels pretty good about having some new friends, but he's not sure these are the kind of friends he needs.
* What might be the consequences if Adam decides to hang out with these guys?
* How can guys appropriately show love for each other?
* How can gang involvement be a substitute for love?
* Should Adam go cruising?

YES   NO   UNDECIDED

Eva

Eva is a fifteen-year-old sophomore. Her dad left her mom three years ago for another woman. Eva lives with her mom, but doesn't spend much time with her—though she'd like to. Her mom always seems too busy with work, Eva's younger brother and sister, or her new boyfriend.

Situation 1: Eva met Matt four months ago at the movies, and since then they've spent all their free time together doing homework, shooting hoops, watching TV, and hanging out with friends. Eva enjoys all the attention, but Matt has started pushing things physically. He told Eva he's never felt this way before, and that if she loves him, she'll have sex with him.

❋ How might Eva and Matt's relationship change if they had sex?
❋ At what point in a relationship is it OK to have sex?
❋ How can sex be a substitute for love?
❋ Should Eva have sex with Matt?

YES   NO   UNDECIDED

Situation 2: Eva's friends Maria and Cathy have been experimenting with drugs. They've invited Eva to a slumber party Friday night so they can get high together. They say it's perfectly safe—Cathy's brother has been doing it for years, and he'll be at home with them. Besides, it's fun.

❋ What might be the consequences if Eva does drugs?
❋ Are there other ways Eva could deal with her family problems?
❋ How can drugs be a substitute for love?
❋ Should Eva go to the sleepover, assuming she'll try drugs if she does?

YES   NO   UNDECIDED

Situation 3: Eva works really hard at getting straight A's in honors classes, and she's also involved in student council. She's proud of her perfect-attendance record and her reputation as the perfect student. But lately, Eva's been feeling a little overweight. Though she knows she's in pretty good shape, she feels that if she were skinnier, life might be better. She carefully watches what she eats and exercises regularly, but lately she feels that all her efforts just aren't paying off.

❋ What might be the consequences of Eva's attitude about her appearance?
❋ What are some appropriate ways to maintain healthy self-esteem?
❋ How can perfectionism be a substitute for love?
❋ Should Eva try to lose weight?

YES   NO   UNDECIDED

Situation 4: Eva loves to shop. Her friends tease her that she buys a new wardrobe every few months, but she just wants to keep up with styles. Eva also collects music and videos. Sometimes she gets money from her mom or her mom's boyfriend, but mostly she sweet-talks her dad out of his cash. She knows he feels guilty about abandoning his family, and she likes having cool stuff. So they're even, right?

❋ What might be the consequences of Eva's attitude toward stuff? toward her dad?
❋ Are there other ways Eva could feel good about herself without having to buy things?
❋ How can materialism be a substitute for love?
❋ Should Eva keep asking her dad for money?

YES   NO   UNDECIDED

why ▼Active and Interactive Learning works with teenagers

Let's Start With the Big Picture

Think back to a major life lesson you've learned.
Got it? Now answer these questions:
● Did you learn your lesson from something you read?
● Did you learn it from something you heard?
● Did you learn it from something you experienced?
If you're like 99 percent of your peers, you answered "yes" only to the third question—you learned your life lesson from something you experienced.

This simple test illustrates the most convincing reason for using active and interactive learning with young people: People learn best through experience. Or to put it even more simply, people learn by doing.

Learning by doing is what active learning is all about. No more sitting quietly in chairs and listening to a speaker expound theories about God—that's passive learning. Active learning gets kids out of their chairs and into the experience of life. With active learning, kids get to *do* what they're studying. They *feel* the effects of the principles you teach. They *learn* by experiencing truth firsthand.

Active learning works because it recognizes three basic learning needs and uses them in concert to enable young people to make discoveries on their own and to find practical life applications for the truths they believe.

So what are these three basic learning needs?
1. Teenagers need action.
2. Teenagers need to think.
3. Teenagers need to talk.
Read on to find out exactly how these needs will be met by using the active and interactive learning techniques in Group's Core Belief Bible Study Series in your youth group.

1. Teenagers Need Action

Aircraft pilots know well the difference between passive and active learning. Their passive learning comes through listening to flight instructors and reading flight-instruction books. Their active learning comes through actually flying an airplane or flight simulator. Books and lectures may be helpful, but pilots really learn to fly by manipulating a plane's controls themselves.

We can help young people learn in a similar way. Though we may engage students passively in some reading and listening to teachers, their understanding and application of God's Word will really take off through simulated and real-life experiences.

Forms of active learning include simulation games; role-plays; service projects; experiments; research projects; group pantomimes; mock trials; construction projects; purposeful games; field trips; and, of course, the most powerful form of active learning—real-life experiences.

We can more fully explain active learning by exploring four of its characteristics:

● **Active learning is an adventure.** Passive learning is almost always predictable. Students sit passively while the teacher or speaker follows a planned outline or script.

In active learning, kids may learn lessons the teacher never envisioned. Because the leader trusts students to help create the learning experience, learners may venture into unforeseen discoveries. And often the teacher learns as much as the students.

● **Active learning is fun and captivating.** What are we communicating when we say, "OK, the fun's over—time to talk about God"? What's the hidden message? That joy is separate from God? And that learning is separate from joy?

What a shame.

Active learning is not joyless. One seventh-grader we interviewed clearly remembered her best Sunday school lesson: "Jesus was the light, and we went into a dark room and shut off the lights. We had a candle, and we learned that Jesus is the light and the dark can't shut off the light." That's active learning. Deena enjoyed the lesson. She had fun. And she learned.

Active learning intrigues people. Whether they find a foot-washing experience captivating or maybe a bit uncomfortable, they learn. And they learn on a level deeper than any work sheet or teacher's lecture could ever reach.

● **Active learning involves everyone.** Here the difference between passive and active learning becomes abundantly clear. It's like the difference between watching a football game on television and actually playing in the game.

The "trust walk" provides a good example of involving everyone in active learning. Half of the group members put on blindfolds; the other half serve as guides. The "blind" people trust the guides to lead them through the building or outdoors. The guides prevent the blind people from falling down stairs or tripping over rocks. Everyone needs to participate to learn the inherent lessons of trust, faith, doubt, fear, confidence, and servanthood. Passive spectators of this experience would learn little, but participants learn a great deal.

● **Active learning is focused through debriefing.** Activity simply for activity's sake doesn't usually result in good learning. Debriefing— evaluating an experience by discussing it in pairs or small groups— helps focus the experience and draw out its meaning. Debriefing helps sort and order the information students gather during the experience. It helps learners relate the recently experienced activity to their lives.

The process of debriefing is best started immediately after an experience. We use a three-step process in debriefing: reflection, interpretation, and application.

Reflection—This first step asks the students, "How did you feel?" Active-learning experiences typically evoke an emotional reaction, so it's appropriate to begin debriefing at that level.

Some people ask, "What do feelings have to do with education?" Feelings have everything to do with education. Think back again to that time in your life when you learned a big lesson. In all likelihood, strong feelings accompanied that lesson. Our emotions tend to cement things into our memories.

When you're debriefing, use open-ended questions to probe feelings. Avoid questions that can be answered with a "yes" or "no." Let your learners know that there are no wrong answers to these "feeling" questions. Everyone's feelings are valid.

Interpretation—The next step in the debriefing process asks, "What does this mean to you? How is this experience like or unlike some other aspect of your life?" Now you're asking people to identify a message or principle from the experience.

You want your learners to discover the message for themselves. So instead of telling students your answers, take the time to ask questions that encourage self-discovery. Use Scripture and discussion in pairs or small groups to explore how the actions and effects of the activity might translate to their lives.

Alert! Some of your people may interpret wonderful messages that you never intended. That's not failure! That's the Holy Spirit at work. God allows us to catch different glimpses of his kingdom even when we all look through the same glass.

Application—The final debriefing step asks, "What will you do about it?" This step moves learning into action. Your young people have shared a common experience. They've discovered a principle. Now they must create something new with what they've just experienced and interpreted. They must integrate the message into their lives.

The application stage of debriefing calls for a decision. Ask your students how they'll change, how they'll grow, what they'll do as a result of your time together.

2. Teenagers Need to Think

Today's students have been trained not to think. They aren't dumber than previous generations. We've simply conditioned them not to use their heads.

You see, we've trained our kids to respond with the simplistic answers they think the teacher wants to hear. Fill-in-the-blank student workbooks and teachers who ask dead-end questions such as "What's the capital of Delaware?" have produced kids and adults who have learned not to think.

And it doesn't just happen in junior high or high school. Our children are schooled very early not to think. Teachers attempt to help kids read with nonsensical fill-in-the-blank drills, word scrambles, and missing-letter puzzles.

Helping teenagers think requires a paradigm shift in how we teach. We need to plan for and set aside time for higher-order thinking and be willing to reduce our time spent on lower-order parroting. Group's Core Belief Bible Study Series is designed to help you do just that.

Thinking classrooms look quite different from traditional classrooms. In most church environments, the teacher does most of the talking and hopes that knowledge will transmit from his or her brain to the students'. In thinking settings, the teacher coaches students to ponder, wonder, imagine, and problem-solve.

3. Teenagers Need to Talk

Everyone knows that the person who learns the most in any class is the teacher. Explaining a concept to someone else is usually more helpful to the explainer than to the listener. So why not let the students do more teaching? That's one of the chief benefits of letting kids do the talking. This process is called interactive learning.

What is interactive learning? Interactive learning occurs when students discuss and work cooperatively in pairs or small groups.

Interactive learning encourages learners to work together. It honors the fact that students can learn from one another, not just from the teacher. Students work together in pairs or small groups to accomplish shared goals. They build together, discuss together, and present together. They teach each other and learn from one another. Success as a group is celebrated. Positive interdependence promotes individual and group learning.

Interactive learning not only helps people learn but also helps learners feel better about themselves and get along better with others. It accomplishes these things more effectively than the independent or competitive methods.

Here's a selection of interactive learning techniques that are used in Group's Core Belief Bible Study Series. With any of these models, leaders may assign students to specific partners or small groups. This will maximize cooperation and learning by preventing all the "rowdies" from linking up. And it will allow for new friendships to form outside of established cliques.

Following any period of partner or small-group work, the leader may reconvene the entire class for large-group processing. During this time the teacher may ask for reports or discoveries from individuals or teams. This technique builds in accountability for the teacherless pairs and small groups.

Pair-Share—With this technique each student turns to a partner and responds to a question or problem from the teacher or leader. Every learner responds. There are no passive observers. The teacher may then ask people to share their partners' responses.

Study Partners—Most curricula and most teachers call for Scripture passages to be read to the whole class by one person. One reads; the others doze.

Why not relinquish some teacher control and let partners read and react with each other? They'll all be involved—and will learn more.

Learning Groups—Students work together in small groups to create a model, design artwork, or study a passage or story; then they discuss what they learned through the experience. Each person in the learning group may be assigned a specific role. Here are some examples:

Reader

Recorder (makes notes of key thoughts expressed during the reading or discussion)

Checker (makes sure everyone understands and agrees with answers arrived at by the group)

Encourager (urges silent members to share their thoughts)

When everyone has a specific responsibility, knows what it is, and contributes to a small group, much is accomplished and much is learned.

Summary Partners—One student reads a paragraph, then the partner summarizes the paragraph or interprets its meaning. Partners alternate roles with each paragraph.

The paraphrasing technique also works well in discussions. Anyone who wishes to share a thought must first paraphrase what the previous person said. This sharpens listening skills and demonstrates the power of feedback communication.

Jigsaw—Each person in a small group examines a different concept, Scripture, or part of an issue. Then each teaches the others in the group. Thus, all members teach, and all must learn the others' discoveries. This technique is called a jigsaw because individuals are responsible to their group for different pieces of the puzzle.

JIGSAW EXAMPLE

Here's an example of a jigsaw.

Assign four-person teams. Have teammates each number off from one to four. Have all the Ones go to one corner of the room, all the Twos to another corner, and so on.

Tell team members they're responsible for learning information in their numbered corners and then for teaching their team members when they return to their original teams.

Give the following assignments to various groups:

Ones: Read Psalm 22. Discuss and list the prophecies made about Jesus.

Twos: Read Isaiah 52:13–53:12. Discuss and list the prophecies made about Jesus.

Threes: Read Matthew 27:1-32. Discuss and list the things that happened to Jesus.

Fours: Read Matthew 27:33-66. Discuss and list the things that happened to Jesus.

After the corner groups meet and discuss, instruct all learners to return to their original teams and report what they've learned. Then have each team determine which prophecies about Jesus were fulfilled in the passages from Matthew.

Call on various individuals in each team to report one or two prophecies that were fulfilled.

You Can Do It Too!

All this information may sound revolutionary to you, but it's really not. God has been using active and interactive learning to teach his people for generations. Just look at Abraham and Isaac, Jacob and Esau, Moses and the Israelites, Ruth and Boaz. And then there's Jesus, who used active learning all the time!

Group's Core Belief Bible Study Series makes it easy for you to use active and interactive learning with your group. The active and interactive elements are automatically built in! Just follow the outlines, and watch as your kids grow through experience and positive interaction with others.

FOR DEEPER STUDY

For more information on incorporating active and interactive learning into your work with teenagers, check out these resources:

● *Why Nobody Learns Much of Anything at Church: And How to Fix It,* by Thom and Joani Schultz (Group Publishing) and

● *Do It! Active Learning in Youth Ministry,* by Thom and Joani Schultz (Group Publishing).

your evaluation of

Bible Study Series
for senior high

why LOVE matters

Group Publishing, Inc.
Attention: Core Belief Talk-Back
P.O. Box 481
Loveland, CO 80539
Fax: (970) 669-1994

Please help us continue to provide innovative and useful resources for ministry. After you've led the studies in this volume, take a moment to fill out this evaluation; then mail or fax it to us at the address above. Thanks!

● ● ● ● ● ● ●

1. As a whole, this book has been (circle one)

not very helpful   very helpful
1   2   3   4   5   6   7   8   9   10

2. The best things about this book:

3. How this book could be improved:

4. What I will change because of this book:

5. Would you be interested in field-testing future Core Belief Bible Studies and giving us your feedback? If so, please complete the information below:

Name _____

Street address _____

City _____ State _____ Zip _____

Daytime telephone (____) _____ Date _____

THANKS!